A PLUME BOOK

T-REX TRIES AGAIN

DR. HUGH MURPHY is a prosthodontist living and practicing in Raleigh, North Carolina. He created *T-Rex Trying* while in dental school and enjoys seeing all the laughter and amusement his books bring to his readers. He loves drawing, painting, fly-fishing, nature, and, most of all, spending time with his family.

T-REX TRIES AGAIN...

RETURN OF THE KING

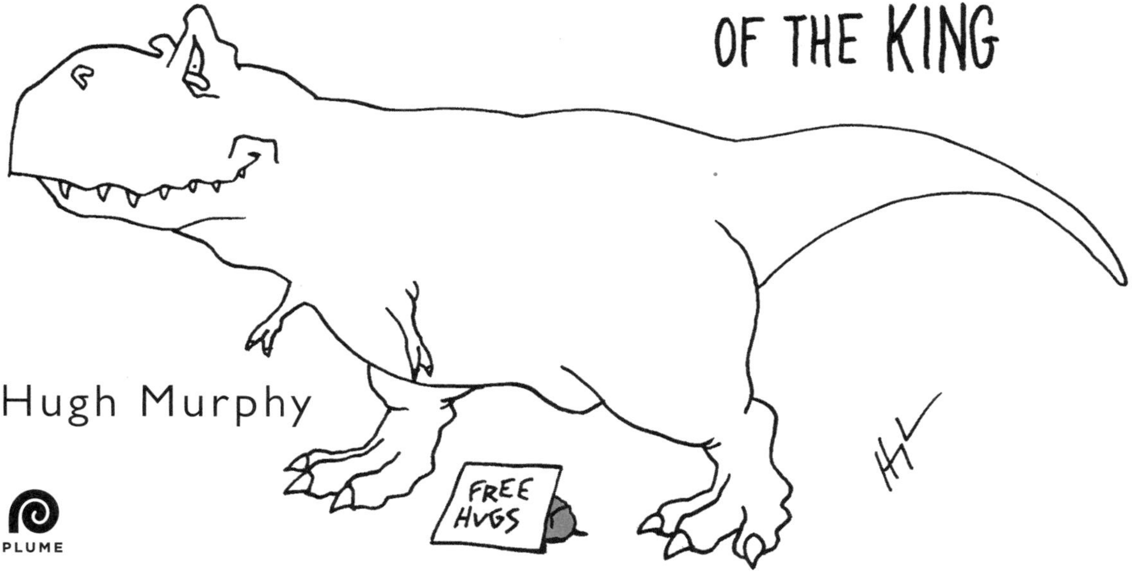
FREE HUGS

Hugh Murphy

PLUME

PLUME
An imprint of Penguin Random House LLC
penguinrandomhouse.com

ISBN 9780593188552 (hardcover)
ISBN 9780593188569 (ebook)

Printed in the United States of America

10 9 8 7 6 5 4 3 2 1

To my parents, my brothers, my wife, my daughters, Pining and Gumer,
and the rest of my friends and family . . .
the truly good things in my life have always come
from the great people in it.

T-REX TRIES AGAIN...

RETURN
OF THE KING

T-Rex trying to find his straw without looking away . . .

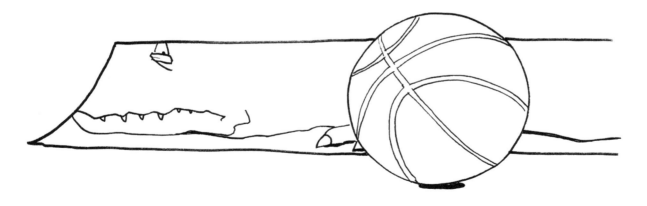

T-Rex trying to fetch a basketball from underneath a car . . .

T-Rex trying to stop a slap shot . . .

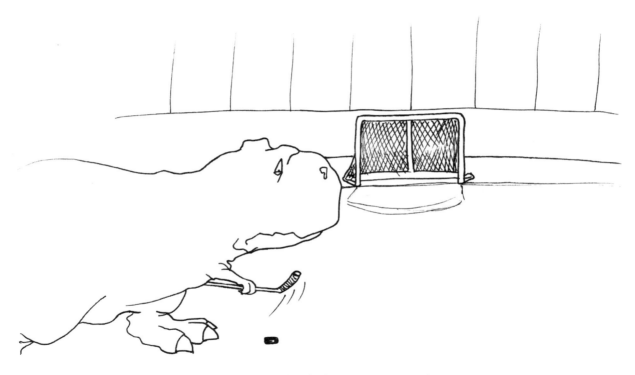

T-Rex trying to take a slap shot . . .

T-Rex trying to play tennis . . .

T-Rex trying to wrap a tiny gift . . .

T-Rex trying to run a food truck . . .

Wee-Rex trying to use a whoopee cushion on T-Rex . . .

T-Rex trying to negotiate the purchase of his "midlife crisis" . . .

T-Rex trying to negotiate the return of his 'midlife crisis' . . .

T-Rex trying to negotiate a baby gate . . .

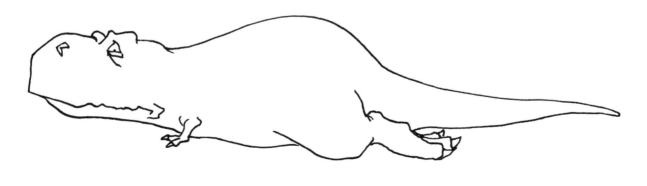

T-Rex trying to do a burpee . . .

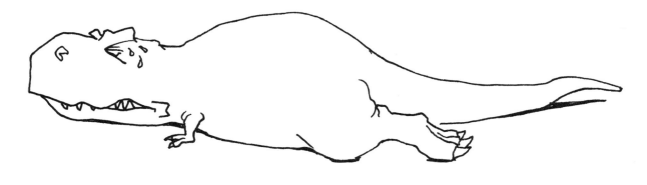

T-Rex really trying to do a burpee . . .

T-Rex still trying to finish a burpee . . .

T-Rex trying to swing a kettlebell . . .

T-Rex trying
to catch fireflies in a jar . . .

T-Rex trying to pull the plug after Wee-Rex's bath . . .

T-Rex trying
fire dancing in Fiji . . .

T-Rex playing the triangle . . .

T-Rex trying to sing 'Itsy Bitsy Spider' with Wee-Rex . . .

T-Rex trying to squish a spider in the corner of the room . . .

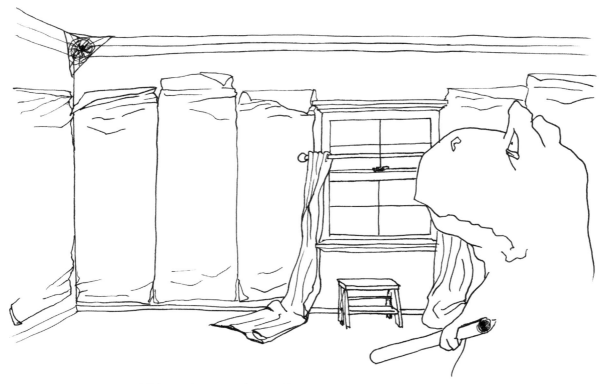

T-Rex trying to wallpaper his living room . . .

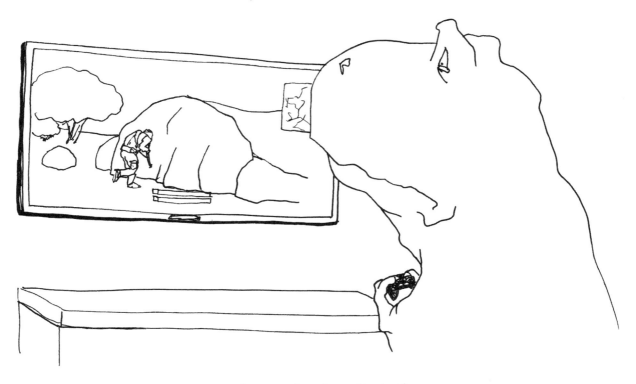

T-Rex trying to play <u>Fortnite</u> . . .

T-Rex trying to stop playing <u>Fortnite</u> . . .

T-Rexes trying to play giant Jenga . . .

T-Rex trying to clean an old chandelier . . .

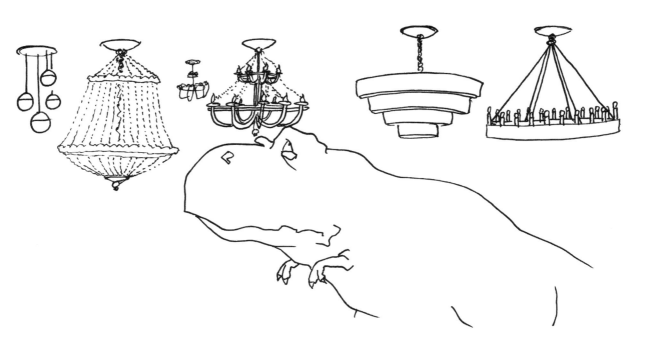

T-Rex trying to buy a new chandelier . . .

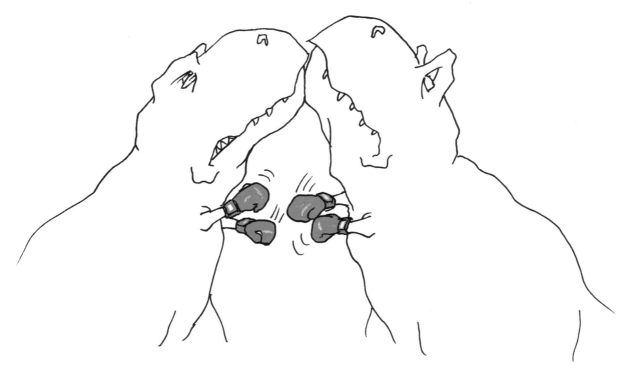

T-Rexes trying to box . . .

T-Rex trying to beatbox . . .

T-Rexes trying to tie water balloons . . .

T-Rex trying to sand wedge out of a bunker . . .

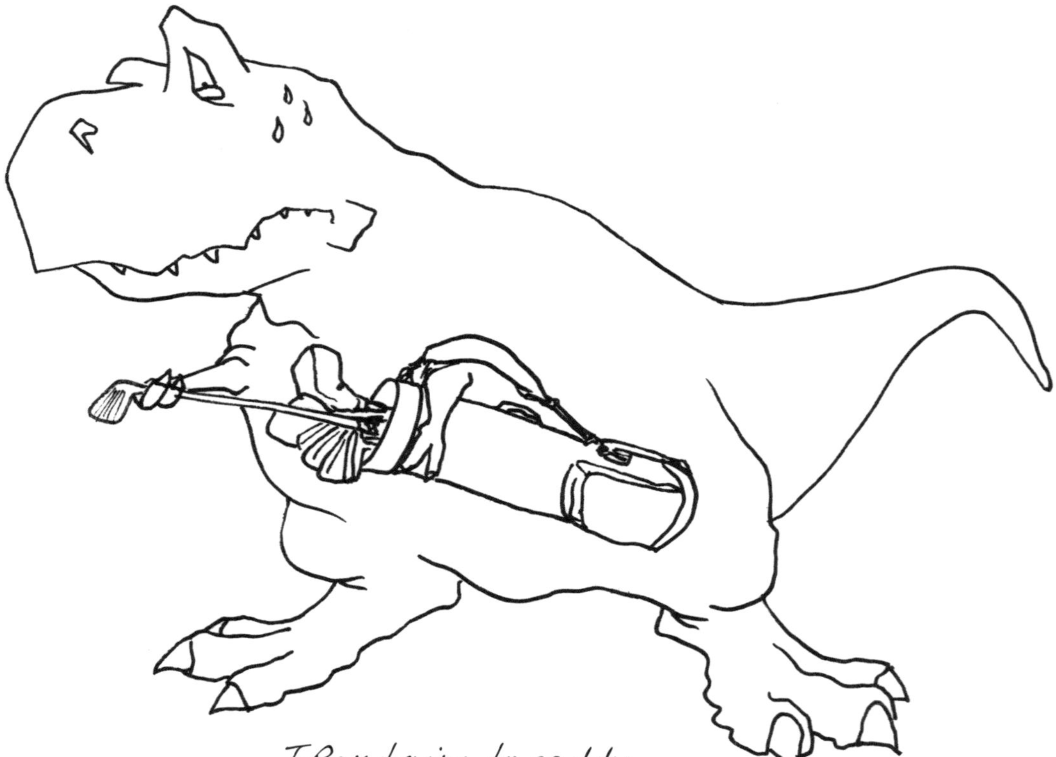

T-Rex trying to caddy . . .

T-Rex trying to play <u>Golden Tee Golf</u> . . .

T-Rex trying to floss . . .

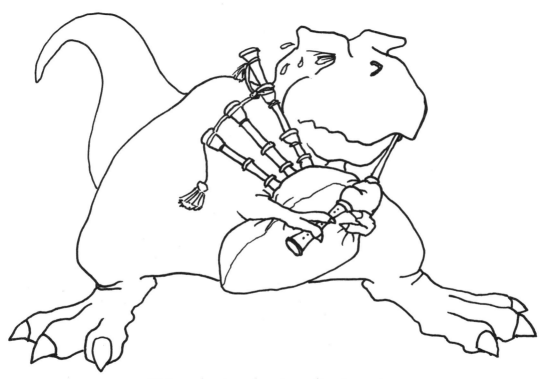

T-Rex trying to play the bagpipes . . .

T-Rex trying to get through TSA at the airport . . .

T-Rex trying to fold a fitted sheet . . .

T-Rex trying to put a comforter into a duvet cover . . .

T-Rex trying to put the duvet on Wee-Rex's new Princess Castle bed . . .

T-Rex trying to make a taco . . .

T-Rex trying to make a taco salad . . .

T-Rex trying to make a martini . . .

T-Rex trying the pommel horse . . .

T-Rex trying to windsurf . . .

T-Rex trying to prune his favorite bonsai tree . . .

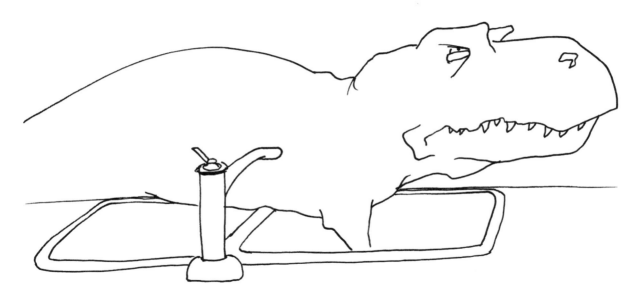

T-Rex trying to clear out the garbage disposal . . .

T-Rex trying to use chopsticks . . .

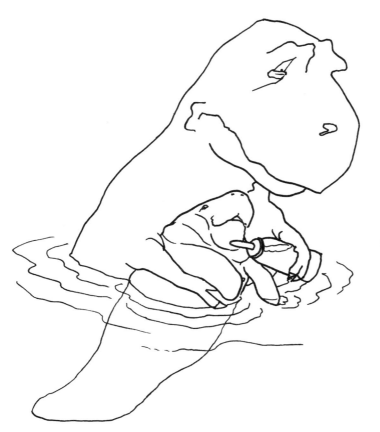

T-Rex trying to nurse
a baby manatee . . .

T-Rex trying to push Wee-Rex on her sled . . .

T-Rex trying to put on a puppet show for Wee-Rex . . .

T-Rexes trying to play Marco Polo . . .

T-Rex trying to win the individual medley . . .

T-Rex trying to win the Assault on <u>American Gladiators</u> . . .

T-Rexes trying to joust on <u>American Gladiators</u> . . .

T-Rex trying to dock a boat . . .

T-Rex trying to plunge a toilet . . .

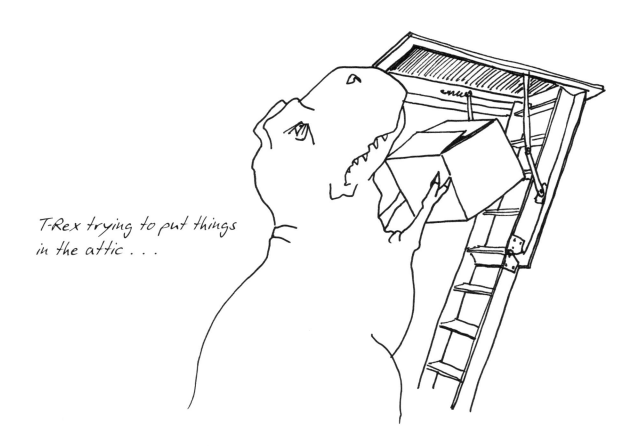

T-Rex trying to put things
in the attic . . .

T-Rex trying to clear cobwebs out of a dusty attic . . .

T-Rex trying to plug in a lamp behind the bed . . .

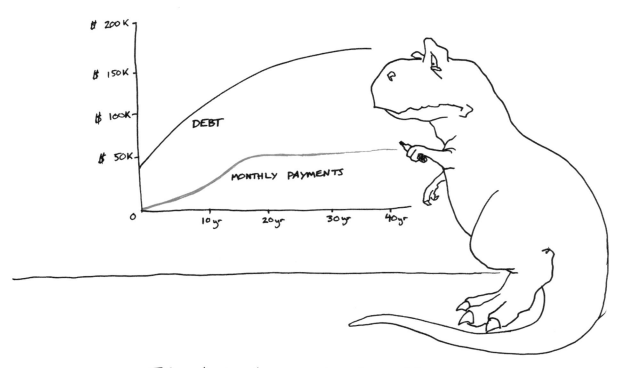

T-Rex trying to repay his student loans . . .

T-Rex trying to put ketchup on his hot dog . . .

T-Rex winning a hot-dog-eating contest . . .

T-Rex bobbing for apples . . .

T-Rex trying to paint a mural of a rainbow . . .

T-Rex trying to draw a giraffe . . .

T-Rex trying to sweep into a dustpan . . .

T-Rex trying to teach a dog to shake . . .

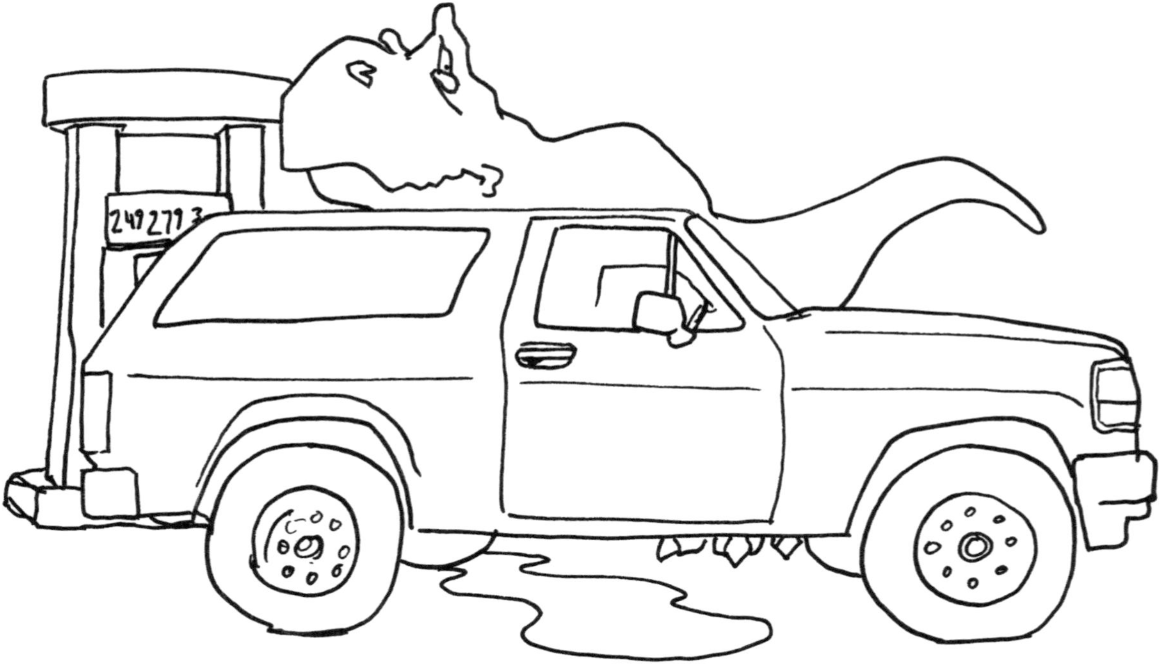
249 279 3

T-Rex trying to pump gas . . .

T-Rex trying to spread out a beach blanket . . .

T-Rex trying to open his beach umbrella . . .

T-Rex trying to chase down his beach umbrella on a windy day . . .

T-Rex trying to catch a wave . . .

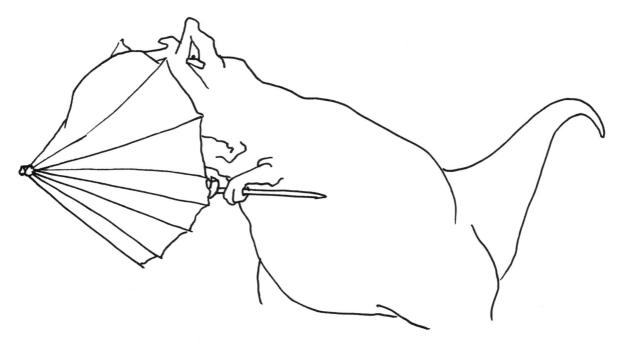

T-Rex trying to close his beach umbrella . . .

T-Rex trying to give a cat a bath . . .

T-Rex trying to direct traffic . . .

T-Rex trying to use crutches . . .

T-Rex trying to use a cane . . .

T-Rex trying to get Wee-Rex out of a bouncy house . . .

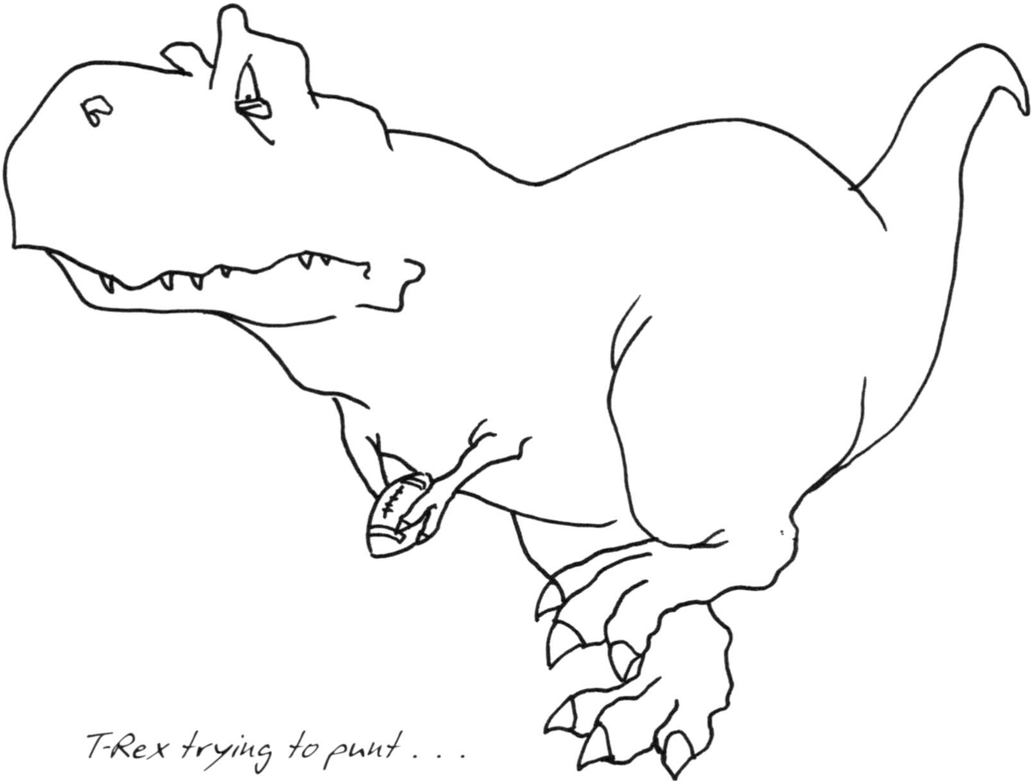

T-Rex trying to punt . . .

T-Rex trying to chop down a tree with an ax . . .

T-Rex trying to cut down a tree with a chain saw . . .

T-Rexes trying to cut down a tree using a two-person saw . . .

T-Rex trying to feed a horse through an electric fence . . .

T-Rexes trying to make pizza . . .

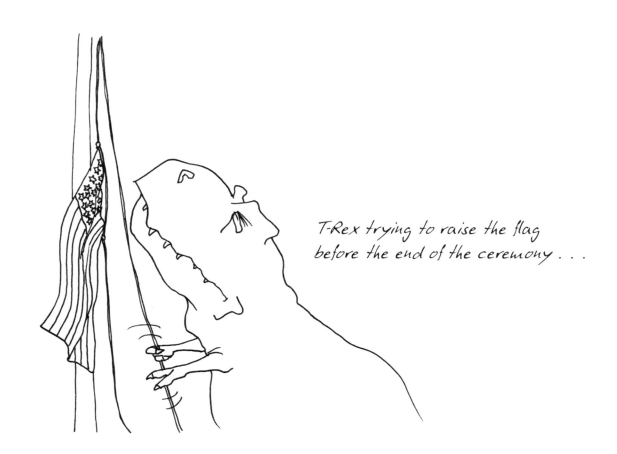

T-Rex trying to raise the flag before the end of the ceremony . . .

T-Rexes trying to have a thumb war . . .

T-Rex trying to shear
a flock of sheep . . .

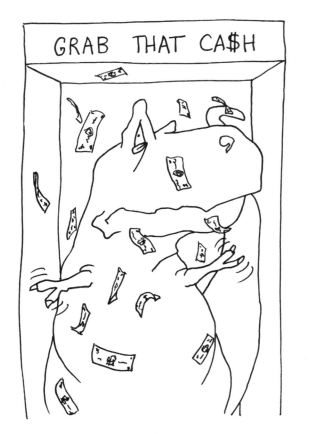

T-Rex trying to grab cash in a windy booth . . .

T-Rex trying to grab the toys
at the bottom of the pool . . .

T-Rex trying to light a gas fireplace . . .

T-Rex trying to panhandle . . .

T-Rex trying to get the first scoop of ice cream . . .

T-Rex trying to mine for gems . . .

T-Rex trying to pan for gold . . .

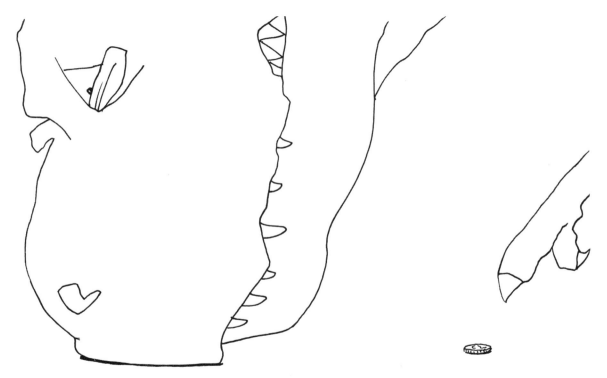

T-Rex trying to pick up a lucky penny . . .

T-Rex trying
to rent a car . . .

T-Rex trying to hustle pedestrians as a street performer . . .

T-Rex trying to hail a cab . . .

T-Rex trying to show Wee-Rex that tiny arms can be graceful too . . .

Wee-Rex trying to show T-Rex
that tiny arms can give
great hugs too . . .

ALSO BY HUGH MURPHY

T-REX TRYING...
Hugh Murphy

9780452299023

T-REX TRYING
AND TRYING
The unfortunate trials
of a modern prehistoric
family
HUGH MURPHY

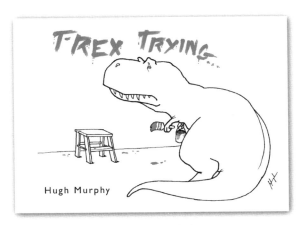

9780142181706